Robert Redfo
The Rebel Behind The

Edward B. Steele

Copyright
All rights reserved. No part of this publication may be reproduced, distributed, or transmitted in any form or by any means, including photocopying, recording, or other electronic or mechanical methods, without the prior written permission of the publisher, except in the case of brief quotations embodied in critical reviews and certain other noncommercial uses permitted by copyright law.
Copyright © Edward B. Steele 2025
Disclaimer
This book is an independent, unofficial biography. It is not authorized, endorsed, licensed, or approved by the individual, their family, representatives, or affiliated entities.
All information contained in this publication is based on publicly available sources, journalistic research, and personal interpretation. The author and publisher have made every effort to ensure factual accuracy and fair representation at the time of publication.
This work is intended for educational and informational purposes only. Names, trademarks, and images that may appear in this book are the property of their respective owners and are used in a descriptive and editorial context only.
If any individual or organization believes this book infringes upon their rights, they are encouraged to contact the publisher directly for immediate review and resolution.
Table of Content

Chapter 1

Introduction
Robert Redford is one of those rare figures whose life and career seem to stretch far beyond the boundaries of Hollywood. He is a man whose name has become synonymous with American cinema, yet his story is not only about fame and movies but also about

passion, vision, activism, and the pursuit of purpose. When people hear his name, they might first think of the classic films "Butch Cassidy and the Sundance Kid," "The Sting," "All the President's Men," or "Out of Africa." They might picture his iconic smile, his natural charisma, and his ability to bring authenticity to the roles he played. But Robert Redford's legacy goes much deeper. He is not just a movie star. He is an actor, a director, a producer, a champion for independent film, and a lifelong activist for environmental and social causes. His story is one of a man who never settled for being only what the industry expected him to be. Instead, he carved his own path, often at great risk, and changed the face of modern cinema in the process.

Redford's life journey began far from the glamorous world of Hollywood. He grew up in a modest household, learning early on about hard work, resilience, and the importance of creativity. His childhood was marked by both struggles and opportunities, and like many great artists, he faced moments of uncertainty that could have led him down entirely different paths. There was a time when his dream was not to become an actor at all, but to express himself through painting. Art was his first passion, and it remained a part of his spirit even when the world knew him primarily as a leading man. That background in painting shaped his vision, his eye for detail, and his ability to see stories not just as scripts but as living canvases. This artistic foundation would later influence his work behind the camera, making him not just an actor but a storyteller of remarkable depth.

As he entered the world of acting, Redford encountered the challenges that all young performers face: rejection, uncertainty, and the constant pressure to fit into Hollywood's narrow mold of stardom. But Redford had something unique. He was not willing to be defined solely by his looks or the roles others wanted him to play. He sought out projects that mattered to him, that spoke to deeper truths about human nature and society. That determination to be more than a Hollywood product set him apart. His choices of roles often reflected a balance between mass appeal and meaningful storytelling. Whether playing charming con men, daring outlaws, or journalists uncovering corruption, he brought intelligence and authenticity to every character. Audiences connected with him not only because of his screen presence but because he always seemed real, grounded, and human.

But it was not enough for him to be in front of the camera. Redford had the vision and courage to step into roles as a director and producer, where he could shape the kinds of stories that were told. His directorial debut, "Ordinary People," proved that he was not only a capable filmmaker but also a deeply insightful one. The film earned him an Academy Award for Best Director and demonstrated his gift for exploring the complexities of human relationships. This was no small achievement. Many actors who try to move into directing struggle to find the same success, but Redford made the transition with remarkable grace. His films as a director often carried his signature qualities: sensitivity, authenticity, and a refusal to shy away from difficult themes. He became a filmmaker who told stories that mattered, who sought to reveal truths about the human condition.

Yet perhaps one of Robert Redford's greatest contributions to the world of cinema has nothing to do with his performances or even his directing. It is the creation of the Sundance Film Festival. At a time when Hollywood was dominated by big studios, formulaic blockbusters, and commercial priorities, Redford recognized that independent filmmakers needed a space to be seen and heard. Sundance began as a small idea, a gathering that would give independent voices a platform. Over time, it grew into one of the most important film festivals in the world, a launching pad for countless directors, writers, and actors who might otherwise have been overlooked. Through Sundance, Redford helped reshape the landscape of film, ensuring that diversity of voice and originality had a place alongside mainstream cinema. This is perhaps his most lasting gift to the industry, a legacy that continues to influence generations of filmmakers.

But Redford's life has not been limited to art and film. He has always been deeply committed to activism, particularly environmental issues. Long before it became fashionable or widely accepted, Redford used his platform to speak out about the need to protect nature, conserve resources, and recognize the urgent threat of climate change. He lent his voice, his time, and his influence to causes that mattered, often at the risk of criticism. To him, the environment was not just a cause but a responsibility. Growing up with an appreciation for the natural world, he carried that respect into his adult life, advocating for policies and practices that would safeguard the planet for future generations. His activism reflected the same qualities that defined his career: courage, independence, and a refusal to remain silent in the face of injustice.

At the same time, his personal life has been marked by complexity and depth. He has known the joy of family and the pain of personal loss. He has balanced the demands of fame with the desire for privacy. Despite being one of the most recognizable faces in the world, Redford has often sought to live quietly, away from the glare of constant publicity. This balance between public life and personal retreat speaks to his character. He has always valued authenticity over image, substance over spectacle. Even as Hollywood celebrated him as a star, he remained grounded in his values, often retreating to his home in the mountains, where he could find peace in the natural world he loved.

When considering Robert Redford's life, one cannot separate the man from the values he represents. His story is not only about the movies he made or the awards he won. It is about a commitment to art, to truth, to independence, and to making a difference in the world. His career has spanned decades, touching on some of the most important moments in American cultural history. From the political upheavals of the 1970s, reflected in films like "All the President's Men," to the rise of independent cinema through Sundance, Redford has always been at the center of meaningful change. His work resonates not just because it entertains but because it challenges, inspires, and reminds us of what cinema can achieve.

Early Life and Childhood

Robert Redford's early life and childhood shaped the man who would later become one of the most influential figures in American cinema. To understand his journey, it is important to return to the years before he was a star, when he was just a boy growing up in a working-class family, learning about hardship, resilience, and the beauty of creativity. These years were not glamorous. They were filled with the ordinary struggles and experiences of a child in mid-20th century America, yet from those beginnings, Redford's character, imagination, and independence were born.

He was born Charles Robert Redford Jr. on August 18, 1936, in Santa Monica, California, just a short distance from Hollywood. At that time, Santa Monica was not the bustling, wealthy city it is known as today. It was a quieter place, with wide streets, modest neighborhoods, and a strong sense of community. His family lived in a modest home, far from the glamour of the film studios nearby. His father, Charles Redford Sr., worked as a milkman and later as an accountant. His mother, Martha Hart, was a homemaker whose warmth and encouragement would leave a lasting impact on her son. Redford grew up with a sense of discipline from his father, who was strict and practical, and with love and imagination from his mother, who believed in dreams and possibilities.

The world Robert was born into was one of uncertainty. The Great Depression had left deep scars on American families, and although his birth came a few years after its worst years, its effects were still felt in households across the nation. Families like the Redfords knew the meaning of hard work and sacrifice. This atmosphere instilled in young Robert an understanding that life was not always easy and that perseverance mattered. Yet despite the challenges, there was also joy in his home. His parents believed in family and in creating a foundation of values that would guide him throughout his life.

Robert's childhood was marked by a blend of structure and freedom. His father, with his stern but steady personality, expected him to be responsible, disciplined, and hardworking. His mother, on the other hand, was more nurturing and encouraged Robert to think creatively. She believed in his talents, even when they were raw and uncertain, and she gave him the confidence to imagine possibilities beyond the ordinary. This balance between the practical and the imaginative would later define Redford's personality, making him both grounded and visionary.

As a boy, Robert was full of energy and curiosity. He was not always the most disciplined student. School, with its rules and routines, did not always capture his attention. Teachers often saw him as restless, sometimes even as a child who struggled to focus. But outside the classroom, he thrived. He was fascinated by drawing and painting, finding joy in expressing himself through art. He would sketch and imagine, creating worlds that allowed him to escape from the ordinary rhythms of everyday life. This love of art was more than just a childhood hobby—it became his first true passion. He dreamed of becoming an artist, of one day traveling the world and living a life devoted to creativity. That dream, though it would later shift toward acting and film, never completely left him. Even as an adult, painting remained an essential part of his identity.

Sports were another important part of his childhood. Growing up in California, he spent much of his time outdoors. He played baseball and developed a love for physical activity. Baseball, in particular, became a meaningful outlet for him. It gave him discipline, teamwork, and the thrill of competition. He was good at it, too, and for a time, he considered the possibility of pursuing it more seriously. Baseball provided him with a sense of belonging and confidence that he did not always find in the classroom.

But childhood was not without its hardships. When Robert was a teenager, tragedy struck his family. His mother, who had always been his greatest source of encouragement, died in 1955 from a hemorrhage after surgery. Robert was only 18 years old at the time, and the loss left a profound mark on him. He was deeply attached to her, and her death created a sense of emptiness that stayed with him throughout his life. It also gave him a strong sense of independence. Without her presence to guide him, he felt the need to carve his own path and find meaning in his own way. That experience of loss shaped his outlook, making him both more introspective and more determined to live fully.

During his adolescence, Redford also struggled with questions of identity and belonging. He was not the perfect student, nor did he follow a straightforward path. At times, he felt like an outsider, unsure of exactly where he fit. He dabbled in mischief and rebellion, sometimes drinking too much and drifting away from the expectations others had for him. These moments of restlessness, while troubling for his family, were also part of his search for freedom. He did not want to be confined by rigid rules or limited dreams. He yearned for something larger, something that allowed him to express himself and to live authentically.

After high school, Redford's path was uncertain. He attended the University of Colorado on a baseball scholarship, but he did not remain there long. College life, with its structure and responsibilities, did not suit him at the time. He dropped out, a decision that at first seemed reckless but ultimately opened the door to a different journey. Instead of following a conventional path, he traveled. He went to Europe, where he immersed himself in art, culture, and self-discovery. In Paris and Florence, he studied painting, lived simply, and soaked in the atmosphere of a different world. These years abroad were formative. They gave him a broader perspective on life, exposed him to new ideas, and allowed him to see himself not just as a boy from California but as someone with the potential to shape his own destiny.

His early experiences in art and travel gave him a strong sense of individuality. They taught him that there was more to life than security and routine. He learned to value creativity, risk, and vision. Those lessons would later fuel his career in acting and directing, where he constantly sought to balance commercial success with meaningful storytelling. They also gave him a respect for authenticity, a quality that would make his performances stand out in Hollywood.

Looking back on Robert Redford's childhood and early years, it is clear that they were a time of contrast—between discipline and rebellion, hardship and joy, loss and discovery. They were not easy years, but they were formative. The boy who grew up in a modest California neighborhood, who loved baseball, who dreamed of being an artist, and who lost his beloved mother too soon, would later channel all those experiences into his work. His ability to portray characters with depth and vulnerability, his passion for art, and his drive to create space for independent voices in film can all be traced back to those early foundations.

What stands out most about Redford's early life is the way he embraced both struggle and imagination. He was not shaped by privilege or by a smooth path. Instead, he grew through adversity, through trial and error, through exploration and risk. That journey gave him a resilience and a perspective that would serve him well in the unpredictable world of Hollywood. His story reminds us that greatness often begins not with certainty or perfection but with the willingness to search, to dream, and to persevere.

Discovering His Passion for Art and Acting

Robert Redford's journey into the world of art and acting was neither direct nor predictable. It was a path shaped by curiosity, rebellion, and the desire to express something within himself that ordinary life could not contain. From a young age, he was drawn to creativity, but he did not yet know what form that creativity would take. Art was his first love, a discipline that allowed him to translate feelings into images. Acting came later, almost by accident, but when it arrived, it opened doors that changed the course of his life forever. To understand the man he became, it is important to look closely at the period in which he discovered his passions and began shaping them into a career.

As a boy in Santa Monica, Redford often felt restless. He was not the type of student who thrived in traditional classrooms. Rules, memorization, and repetition did little to inspire him. But he had a natural eye for detail and a sensitivity to the world around him. He could see things differently, noticing textures, colors, and moods in ways others often overlooked. Drawing and painting became an outlet for this sensitivity. With a pencil or brush in hand, he could capture the emotions he struggled to express in words. His art was not about perfection but about exploration, a way of making sense of both the beauty and the confusion of life.

The discipline of art gave him a sense of purpose. While his peers were consumed by sports or school activities, Redford was more interested in sketching faces, experimenting with lines, and studying shadows. His mother supported this early interest, encouraging him to follow his instincts rather than force himself into molds that did not fit. In many ways, she gave him permission to dream. She believed in the value of creativity, even when others might have dismissed it as impractical. This encouragement planted the seed of confidence that would later carry him through rejection and doubt.

In high school, Redford's artistic inclinations were sometimes overshadowed by his love of baseball. He was talented enough to earn a scholarship to the University of Colorado, where he hoped to balance academics with athletics. But while baseball offered him a structure and a team, art continued to tug at him in quieter but stronger ways. College life, however, was not a perfect fit. Redford struggled with discipline and with the expectations placed upon him. His time at the university was marked more by restlessness than by achievement, and eventually, he lost his scholarship. What might have seemed like a failure at the time was, in truth, the beginning of his real education.

After leaving the University of Colorado, Redford's path turned toward Europe. This was a pivotal decision, one that reflected his deep need to explore beyond the boundaries of American life. In Paris, Florence, and other European cities, he immersed himself in art. He attended classes, visited museums, and allowed himself to absorb the atmosphere of centuries-old traditions. For a young man from California, the experience was transformative. Europe opened his eyes to a world where art was not a hobby but a way of life, where creativity was central to culture. Walking through the streets of Paris or sitting in the piazzas of Florence, he began to see himself not as a failed athlete or a restless student but as an artist searching for his voice.

Those years abroad were filled with both discipline and freedom. He studied painting seriously, working to refine his technique and to understand the masters who had come before him. At the same time, he lived with the kind of freedom only a young traveler can know—working odd jobs, living modestly, and observing life with an artist's eye. These experiences taught him resilience. He learned to live simply, to rely on his own resourcefulness, and to find inspiration in the smallest details of daily life. The world was his classroom, and he absorbed it with a hunger that would later fuel his performances as an actor.

When he returned to the United States, Redford carried with him not only the skills he had developed as a painter but also a broader vision of what it meant to live creatively. Yet life at home brought new challenges. His father, practical and disciplined, did not always understand his son's artistic ambitions. Redford, however, was no longer content with the idea of settling into a conventional job or lifestyle. He wanted something more, something that allowed him to express the complexity of his experiences.

It was around this time that acting began to emerge as a possibility. At first, it was not a deliberate choice but rather a suggestion, an experiment, a way of trying something new. Redford enrolled at the American Academy of Dramatic Arts in New York City, where he began to study the craft of acting. To his surprise, he found that the skills he had developed as an artist observation, attention to detail, sensitivity to mood translated seamlessly into performance. Acting, like painting, required seeing beneath the surface, capturing not only appearances but the emotions and truths hidden underneath. In the theater classrooms of New York, Redford discovered a new kind of canvas. Instead of brushes and paint, he had words, movement, and expression. Instead of a blank page, he had a stage. Acting demanded vulnerability, discipline, and imagination, qualities that Redford was beginning to cultivate. He found the work challenging, but also exhilarating. For the first time, he felt a sense of direction that combined his artistic instincts with a new form of expression.

The stage soon became his proving ground. In New York, he performed in small plays, gradually learning the craft and building his confidence. Acting was not about fame at this stage; it was about discovery. He watched other actors closely, studied their techniques, and absorbed everything he could. His art background gave him a unique perspective. He saw characters as layered and complex, like portraits waiting to be painted with words and gestures. He understood the importance of subtlety, of what could be conveyed not by dialogue but by silence, posture, and the smallest flicker of expression.

What made acting so appealing to him was its immediacy. Painting required solitude, long hours in front of a canvas, and often, a distance between the artist and the audience. Acting, however, was alive, present, and shared. It allowed him to connect with people in a direct and powerful way. When he stepped onto a stage or later in front of a camera, he felt the energy of that connection. It was art in motion, art that breathed and responded. This realization ignited something in him that painting alone could not fulfill.

As he gained more experience, Redford began to see acting as not just a skill but a calling. It gave him the opportunity to inhabit lives beyond his own, to explore human nature in all its complexity. Each role became a journey into another world, another perspective, another truth. He understood that through acting, he could tell stories that mattered, stories that reflected both the struggles and the beauty of being human.

His time in New York was crucial not only for his growth as an actor but also for his understanding of discipline. Acting was not simply about talent; it was about work, preparation, and constant refinement. He threw himself into the craft, learning from teachers, fellow students, and his own mistakes. Slowly, he began to build a reputation, and opportunities started to come his way.

The transition from art to acting did not mean abandoning painting. In many ways, his work as an actor was an extension of his identity as an artist. The same eye for detail that guided his brushstrokes now guided his performances. The same desire to express emotions visually now found expression in his gestures and expressions on stage. Painting had given him the foundation; acting gave him the stage on which to expand it.

It is clear that Redford's discovery of acting was not a sudden event but the result of years of searching, experimenting, and refining his creative instincts. From his childhood sketches in Santa Monica, to his studies in Europe, to his training in New York, each step prepared him for the next. What made him different from many of his peers was his refusal to settle. He did not accept the idea of fitting into a conventional mold. Instead, he pursued what inspired him, even when it seemed impractical or uncertain. That determination to follow his passion was the key to his later success.

By the time he began to gain recognition in the acting world, Robert Redford had already lived a life rich with experience, loss, exploration, and discovery. He was not just another young man chasing fame; he was an artist who had found a new medium. Acting allowed him to combine his sensitivity, his eye for truth, and his need for expression into a career that would eventually touch millions of lives. His passion for art had led him naturally to acting, and together, they became the foundation of a life devoted to creativity.

Chapter 2

Breaking into Hollywood

After his studies at the American Academy of Dramatic Arts in New York, Redford began his career in the theater, which became the first real stage for his talent. He performed in small productions, building his craft and his reputation in front of live audiences. Acting in theater taught him discipline, precision, and the ability to carry a character night after night, lessons that would serve him well later in film. He began to attract attention for his good looks and natural charisma, but it was his seriousness as an actor that helped him stand out. He did not treat acting as a superficial pursuit but as an art, and even at the beginning, he insisted on bringing depth to his roles.

The stage eventually opened the door to television. In the late 1950s and early 1960s, American television was booming, offering actors opportunities to appear in live dramas and episodic series. Redford began making guest appearances on popular shows such as "Maverick," "Perry Mason," "The Twilight Zone," and "Alfred Hitchcock Presents." These roles were small, often one-off characters, but they gave him valuable screen experience and introduced him to a wider audience. For many young actors, television was simply a stepping stone, but for Redford, it was also a way to explore different kinds of characters and to prove that he could adapt to the demands of the camera.

Television work also revealed something important about him: he was not content with surface-level performances. Even when the scripts were limited, he tried to bring authenticity to his roles. He observed, listened, and studied how people behaved in real life, then used those observations to shape his characters. It was this attention to detail that began to separate him from other aspiring actors. Viewers noticed, casting directors noticed, and slowly his reputation began to grow.

His first real breakthrough came on the stage, however, with his role in Neil Simon's Broadway hit *Barefoot in the Park* in 1963. Redford played Paul Bratter, a young lawyer newly married to a free-spirited woman played by Elizabeth Ashley. The play was a massive success, running for over 1,500 performances, and Redford's performance drew rave reviews. It showcased his ability to balance charm, wit, and emotional honesty, and it made him a recognizable name in the theater world. For an actor still searching for his place, this was an important turning point. Broadway gave him the visibility and credibility he needed to catch Hollywood's attention.

Hollywood, of course, was quick to notice Redford's good looks. With his blond hair, blue eyes, and athletic build, he fit the mold of the classic leading man that studios often sought. Yet Redford was wary of being typecast. He did not want to be seen merely as a handsome face. He wanted roles that allowed him to explore complex emotions and to play characters with depth. This tension between Hollywood's desire to package him and his own desire for authenticity would define much of his early career.

His first significant film role came in *War Hunt* (1962), a low-budget war movie in which he played a young soldier. The film itself was modest, but it introduced him to the mechanics of movie-making and to the realities of Hollywood production. More importantly, it confirmed his belief that cinema could be a powerful medium for storytelling. Unlike the fleeting nature of television or the repetitive cycle of theater, film offered the chance to create something lasting, something that could reach audiences around the world.

Despite his ambitions, Redford's early years in Hollywood were filled with uncertainty. He took roles in films that did not always reflect his full potential. Movies like Inside Daisy Clover (1965) and The Chase (1966) gave him exposure but did not quite establish him as a major star. He was praised for his performances, but the films themselves were uneven, and Redford often felt frustrated by the lack of control he had over his career. Still, each role gave him experience, and each project built his reputation a little further.

The turning point came in 1967 when Redford reprised his Broadway role in the film adaptation of Barefoot in the Park, this time opposite Jane Fonda. The film was a hit, and Redford's performance confirmed that he could carry a movie as a leading man. Audiences loved his chemistry with Fonda, and critics noted that he brought warmth and depth to what could have been a simple romantic comedy role. This was the moment when Hollywood began to see him not just as a supporting player but as a bankable star.

Still, Redford remained cautious. He understood the dangers of being locked into light romantic roles. He wanted more. His instincts proved correct, because just two years later, in 1969, he landed the role that would change his career forever: the Sundance Kid in Butch Cassidy and the Sundance Kid. Starring opposite Paul

Newman, Redford brought charm, humor, and quiet intensity to the role of the outlaw partner in one of the most iconic buddy films in cinema history. The movie was a huge success, both critically and commercially, and it cemented Redford's status as a Hollywood star.

What made Butch Cassidy and the Sundance Kid so important was not just its success but the way it aligned with Redford's sensibilities. The film was witty, stylish, and unconventional, breaking away from the traditional Western formula. Redford's Sundance Kid was not just a handsome sidekick but a fully realized character, blending lightheartedness with depth. His performance alongside Newman created one of the most memorable partnerships in film history, and their chemistry on screen set a new standard for buddy films. For Redford, it was proof that he could take risks, trust his instincts, and succeed.

From that point on, Hollywood opened its doors wide for him. Offers poured in, and he had the freedom to choose projects more carefully. He starred in Downhill Racer (1969) and Tell Them Willie Boy Is Here (1969), both films that reflected his desire to explore complex characters and meaningful themes. Unlike many stars who were content to ride the wave of commercial success, Redford deliberately sought out films that challenged him and pushed boundaries.

Breaking into Hollywood, then, was not simply a matter of being discovered. For Robert Redford, it was a process of negotiation between what the industry wanted from him and what he wanted from himself. He had to prove that he was more than just a handsome face, more than just a conventional leading man. He had to show that he could bring depth, intelligence, and authenticity to his roles. And he succeeded.

By the early 1970s, Redford was not only one of the most bankable stars in Hollywood but also one of its most respected. He had carefully navigated the transition from theater to television to film, never losing sight of his artistic values. His rise was built not on luck alone but on years of preparation, discipline, and a refusal to compromise his vision.

In breaking into Hollywood, Redford also laid the foundation for the rest of his career. His early choices revealed a pattern that would continue throughout his life: a constant balancing act between commercial success and meaningful art, between the demands of the industry and his own sense of purpose. He would go on to become not only a star but also a director, producer, and founder of the Sundance Film Festival, continuing the work of expanding cinema beyond the limitations he had fought against in his early years.

Rise to Stardom: Iconic Movie Roles

His breakthrough came with roles that combined good looks with genuine substance. Films such as "Inside Daisy Clover" (1965) and "This Property Is Condemned" (1966), in which he starred opposite Natalie Wood, introduced him to audiences as more than a passing pretty face. These roles showed his ability to bring nuance and emotional weight to characters, even if the films themselves were not massive successes. Audiences began to notice him, and more importantly, directors saw potential in him as someone who could bring both depth and broad appeal to a project. His early successes laid the groundwork for what would come in the late 1960s and 1970s, a period when Redford would ascend to superstardom.

The turning point was undeniably his role in "Butch Cassidy and the Sundance Kid" (1969). Paired with Paul Newman, who was already a Hollywood heavyweight, Redford played the Sundance Kid with a blend of charm, wit, and understated toughness that perfectly balanced Newman's flamboyant Butch Cassidy. The film was not only a box office triumph but also a cultural phenomenon, cementing Redford as a leading man of the highest order. The easy camaraderie and banter between Newman and Redford captivated audiences, creating one of cinema's most memorable duos. It was here that Redford's image as the golden boy of Hollywood took full shape, though he was always keenly aware of the dangers of being confined to that identity.

Following the success of "Butch Cassidy and the Sundance Kid," Redford quickly capitalized on his new status. He continued to choose roles that had mainstream appeal but also carried a degree of complexity. In "Downhill Racer" (1969), he played a ruthless, ambitious skier whose drive for success highlighted the darker side of competitive sports and personal ambition. Though the film was more of a critical than commercial success, it showed Redford's willingness to step into roles that weren't always flattering, demonstrating a desire to explore human flaws rather than just rely on charm. Similarly, "Tell Them Willie Boy Is Here" (1969) showcased his interest in stories that questioned American myths and history, a theme he would return to throughout his career.

The 1970s marked the height of Redford's superstardom, as he anchored a string of iconic films that became synonymous with his name. In "Jeremiah Johnson" (1972), he took on the role of a rugged mountain man, portraying isolation and survival with a quiet intensity that resonated with audiences seeking stories of independence and self-reliance in a turbulent era. Then came "The Candidate" (1972), where he played an idealistic lawyer turned reluctant politician. The film tapped into the cynicism and disillusionment of American politics at the time, and Redford's performance was both convincing and timely, reinforcing his reputation as an actor who could embody the anxieties and aspirations of his generation.

Perhaps no film of the decade exemplified his star power better than "The Way We Were" (1973), a sweeping romantic drama in which he starred opposite Barbra Streisand. Redford played the handsome, carefree writer Hubbell Gardiner, whose love affair with Streisand's politically passionate Katie Morosky created one of cinema's most beloved romances. The film's success was immense, and Redford's image as a heartthrob reached new heights. Yet even in a film so defined by romantic fantasy, he brought a subtlety that elevated his character from stereotype into a deeply human figure.

That same year, Redford appeared in "The Sting" (1973), once again alongside Paul Newman. The film, with its intricate con-artist plot and lively period setting, became one of the most beloved films of the era, winning the Academy Award for Best Picture. The chemistry between Newman and Redford was once again electric, and Redford's performance as the young grifter Johnny Hooker earned him his only Academy Award nomination for acting. By this point, he was no longer just a movie star; he was one of the defining faces of 1970s American cinema.

As his fame grew, Redford continued to balance crowd-pleasing roles with projects that carried a social or political edge. In "Three Days of the Condor" (1975), he starred in a tense spy thriller that captured the paranoia of the post-Watergate era. His portrayal of a CIA analyst uncovering corruption within the agency spoke to the public's unease about government transparency and accountability. Similarly, in "All the President's Men" (1976), Redford took on one of his most influential roles as Washington Post journalist Bob Woodward, dramatizing the investigation that uncovered the Watergate scandal. Not only was the film a critical and commercial success, but it also reinforced the importance of journalism and truth at a time when American trust in institutions was faltering. Redford's involvement in the film extended beyond acting; he had been instrumental in acquiring the rights to the story, showing his growing influence as both a creative force and cultural commentator.

What made Redford's rise to stardom so unique was his careful management of his career. Unlike many stars of his era, he was not content to simply ride the wave of his good looks or charm. He consistently sought out roles that challenged him and reflected broader cultural themes. He often played men who, while attractive and likable, were also flawed, conflicted, or caught up in larger systems beyond their control. This refusal to be pigeonholed gave him longevity, ensuring that audiences never tired of seeing him on screen.

By the late 1970s and early 1980s, Redford was firmly entrenched as one of Hollywood's most bankable and respected stars. Films like "The Electric Horseman" (1979), where he played a disillusioned rodeo rider who steals a horse to save it from corporate exploitation, reflected both his star persona and his growing interest in environmental and social issues. Audiences flocked to see him not just because he was Robert Redford, but because his name carried with it a promise of quality and thoughtfulness.

The key to Redford's stardom was his duality: he was both the golden-haired leading man of Hollywood fantasy and a serious actor committed to telling meaningful stories. His career trajectory in the 1960s and 1970s illustrates this balance, as he carefully crafted a body of work that combined mass appeal with intellectual and emotional depth. By the time the 1980s arrived, Redford had not only become one of the most recognizable actors in the world but also a cultural figure who symbolized an era of American cinema defined by both glamour and conscience.

The Sundance Kid and Beyond

Robert Redford's career reached a defining moment when he was cast in the 1969 classic film Butch Cassidy and the Sundance Kid, a role that forever etched him into Hollywood history and gave him an iconic nickname that would follow him throughout his career: "The Sundance Kid." Before this film, Redford was respected as a talented young actor with a few strong performances, but after it, he became a household name and a symbol of a new kind of American leading man. His portrayal of the charming outlaw Sundance, opposite Paul Newman's Butch Cassidy, not only demonstrated his undeniable charisma but also cemented his reputation as one of the most magnetic and versatile actors of his generation. The film's success also marked a turning point in the Hollywood landscape, showcasing a more rebellious, youthful, and stylish kind of cinema that resonated with audiences of the late 1960s and early 1970s. Butch Cassidy and the Sundance Kid was a gamble at the time. Redford was not the first choice for the role; the studio initially wanted a more established star. But Newman, already a major force in Hollywood, saw something special in Redford and insisted on working with him. Their chemistry was undeniable, and what unfolded on screen was more than just a buddy western it was the creation of one of the most beloved on-screen partnerships in cinema history. Redford's quiet intensity played perfectly against Newman's playful energy, and together they brought humor, humanity, and heart to the story of two legendary outlaws. The film became a massive box office success, turning Redford into a bona fide star and providing him with opportunities that would define the next phase of his career.

The role of Sundance also shaped Redford's public image. He became known as the ruggedly handsome, intelligent, and slightly enigmatic figure who could bring depth to roles that might otherwise have been one-dimensional. Unlike many actors who were cast solely for their looks, Redford proved he had the acting chops to embody complex characters, whether they were heroes, antiheroes, or flawed men struggling with inner conflicts. The success of Butch Cassidy and the Sundance Kid was the beginning of a remarkable period in his career, during which he starred in a string of critically acclaimed and commercially successful films that captured the spirit of their times.

In the years that followed, Redford carefully chose projects that showcased both his range and his desire to avoid being typecast. He starred in Downhill Racer (1969), a more introspective and understated film about an ambitious skier, which revealed his preference for layered, character-driven stories. Then came Jeremiah Johnson (1972), a rugged frontier drama in which Redford portrayed a mountain man surviving in the wilderness. This film connected to his own love of nature and the outdoors, foreshadowing the environmental activism that would later define another aspect of his legacy.

But it was The Candidate (1972) that demonstrated his ability to take on contemporary political themes. Playing an idealistic lawyer who reluctantly becomes a politician, Redford captured the disillusionment and cynicism of a generation that had grown weary of politics. His portrayal was both charming and unsettling, showing how ambition and compromise could shape a man's journey in the political arena. The film resonated with audiences and critics alike, reinforcing Redford's growing reputation as an actor who was more than just a pretty face; he was someone who could embody the complexities of American life and culture.

Redford's career trajectory skyrocketed further when he starred in The Sting (1973), once again teaming up with Paul Newman. The film, a stylish caper about two con men, became a massive hit and won the Academy Award for Best Picture. Redford's performance earned him his first and only Academy Award nomination for Best Actor, solidifying his position as one of Hollywood's top stars. His natural chemistry with Newman, combined with his ability to balance charm, wit, and vulnerability, made The Sting a timeless classic.

By this point, Redford was not just a star but an icon of American cinema. His name could carry a film, and his presence drew audiences from around the world. He embodied a new kind of masculinity: sensitive, intelligent, self-assured, and deeply connected to the cultural shifts of the era. While many actors of his generation leaned heavily on macho toughness or detached coolness, Redford offered something different: a blend of strength and introspection that appealed to both men and women.

As the 1970s progressed, Redford's career choices continued to reflect his interest in meaningful stories and cultural relevance. In The Way We Were (1973), he starred opposite Barbra Streisand in a romantic drama that became one of the most beloved films of its time. Playing Hubbell Gardiner, a handsome and privileged man who falls in love with a politically passionate woman, Redford brought depth to a role that could have easily been shallow. The chemistry between him and Streisand was electric, and the film's bittersweet ending left a lasting mark on audiences.

His role in All the President's Men (1976) further cemented his reputation as an actor deeply attuned to the political and social climate of his era. Playing journalist Bob Woodward, who along with Carl Bernstein (played by Dustin Hoffman) investigated the Watergate scandal, Redford captured the urgency and gravity of one of the most significant moments in American history. Beyond acting, Redford was instrumental in bringing the film to the screen, having secured the rights to the journalists' book and pushing for its production. The film became not only a box office hit but also a cultural landmark, highlighting the importance of investigative journalism and the role of the press in holding power accountable.

While these films solidified Redford's legacy as one of the greats, he never allowed himself to be boxed into one type of role. He experimented with a variety of genres and themes, from thrillers like Three Days of the Condor (1975) to lighter fare like Barefoot in the Park (1967), which had showcased his comedic talents earlier in his career. He was equally at home in sweeping dramas, romantic stories, political thrillers, and adventurous tales, proving time and again that his talent transcended boundaries.

The nickname "Sundance Kid" followed him long after the success of Butch Cassidy and the Sundance Kid, but instead of being a limitation, it became a part of his legacy. Redford embraced the name when he later established the Sundance Institute and the Sundance Film Festival in the 1980s, turning it into a symbol of independent cinema and artistic freedom. What began as a role that defined his stardom evolved into a lifelong mission to support new voices and innovative storytelling in film. In this sense, "Sundance" came to represent not only his most famous on-screen persona but also his dedication to shaping the future of the film industry.

Beyond Hollywood, Redford's career in this period also reflected his growing interest in social issues and environmental causes. While audiences adored him for his on-screen roles, he was simultaneously laying the groundwork for a broader impact that extended far beyond acting. His love of nature, evident in films like Jeremiah Johnson, aligned with his environmental advocacy, which would later become central to his public identity.

By the time the 1980s arrived, Robert Redford was more than just a movie star. He was an influential cultural figure whose career choices had helped define an era of American cinema. From Butch Cassidy and the Sundance Kid to All the President's Men His films had entertained millions while also engaging with some of the most pressing issues of the times. His ability to balance commercial success with artistic integrity set him apart from many of his contemporaries and established him as one of the most respected figures in the industry.

Chapter 3

Directing Success: Behind the Camera
Robert Redford's move from in front of the camera to behind it was not a sudden shift but rather a natural extension of his creative curiosity and his desire to explore storytelling in deeper, more

nuanced ways than acting alone allowed. By the time he began directing, Redford had already cemented himself as one of Hollywood's most bankable and admired stars, but that success never dulled his hunger to push boundaries. He understood that cinema was more than star power and box office numbers; it was an art form that could convey powerful messages, illuminate hidden truths, and reach audiences on a profoundly human level. This belief guided him as he transitioned into the director's chair, where he developed a reputation for meticulous craftsmanship, emotional depth, and a willingness to champion stories that other filmmakers might shy away from. His directorial debut, Ordinary People in 1980, instantly proved that Redford was more than just a leading man with good looks and charisma; he was also a filmmaker of remarkable sensitivity and vision. The film, a quiet family drama about grief, guilt, and fractured relationships, was not the kind of flashy blockbuster Hollywood was chasing at the time. Yet Redford recognized its universal resonance and handled the material with restraint and empathy. His decision to direct such a subtle, character-driven story spoke volumes about his priorities as a filmmaker. He was not interested in spectacle for its own sake; he wanted to peel back layers of human emotion and show audiences the fragile, often unspoken struggles that define life. The gamble paid off spectacularly. Ordinary People won four Academy Awards, including Best Picture and Best Director, making Redford one of the few actors to transition seamlessly into directing at such a high level. The success of his debut gave him the credibility to continue directing projects that mattered to him personally rather than merely chasing commercial formulas.

In the years that followed, Redford continued to hone his directorial style, one marked by patience, subtlety, and a deep respect for the complexities of human behavior. Unlike many directors who rely on sweeping camera movements or overtly dramatic flourishes, Redford often preferred stillness, silence, and naturalism. His films were rarely loud or showy; instead, they invited viewers into intimate spaces where characters grappled with difficult questions about identity, morality, and purpose. In The Milagro Beanfield War (1988), his sophomore directorial effort, Redford turned his lens to the struggles of a small New Mexican community fighting to preserve their land and way of life against powerful developers. The film was whimsical at times but also politically pointed, reflecting Redford's lifelong concern for social justice and environmental issues. While it did not achieve the same level of acclaim as

Ordinary People it demonstrated his versatility and his determination to give voice to stories rooted in community, culture, and resistance. One of his most celebrated directing efforts came in 1994 with Quiz Show, a sharp and engrossing drama based on the real-life scandal of rigged television game shows in the 1950s. Redford approached the subject with both precision and depth, exploring not only the corruption at the heart of the scandal but also the broader questions about media, morality, and the hunger for fame. With a stellar cast led by Ralph Fiennes, John Turturro, and Rob Morrow, the film dissected the tension between truth and entertainment, a theme that resonates even more in today's media-saturated world. Quiz Show earned critical acclaim, receiving several Academy Award nominations, and solidified Redford's reputation as a director who could combine entertainment with intellectual and moral inquiry. Another standout moment in his directing career came with A River Runs Through It (1992), based on Norman Maclean's semi-autobiographical novella. The film, starring Brad Pitt and Craig Sheffer, was a meditative exploration of family bonds, spirituality, and the redemptive power of nature, with fly fishing serving as a central metaphor. Redford's treatment of the story was lyrical and poetic, balancing the grandeur of the Montana landscape with the intimate struggles of its characters. His voiceover narration gave the film a timeless quality, and the cinematography, guided by his direction, captured both the physical beauty of the setting and the emotional undercurrents of the narrative. The film was widely praised and remains one of his most beloved works as a director. It also underscored how his environmental passions often intertwined with his cinematic sensibilities, using nature not merely as a backdrop but as an active, almost spiritual presence in the story. Redford's directing success was not confined to nostalgic or historical dramas. In 2010, he directed The Conspirator, a historical legal drama centered on Mary Surratt, the only woman charged in the conspiracy to assassinate Abraham Lincoln. The film was a courtroom drama that probed issues of justice, fairness, and the dangers of sacrificing individual rights for the sake of national security. Although its release was quieter compared to his earlier hits, it revealed Redford's continued interest in projects with moral weight and historical relevance. His films often challenged audiences to think critically about society and their own roles within it, reflecting his conviction that cinema could be a vehicle for social dialogue.

Perhaps what distinguishes Redford most as a director is his ability to draw out powerful performances from his actors. Just as he had been a performer deeply attuned to nuance and authenticity, he extended that same respect to those he directed. Actors often remarked on his collaborative style and the sense of trust he fostered on set. He did not micromanage or dominate; instead, he created an environment where performers felt free to explore and inhabit their roles fully. This collaborative spirit not only enhanced the quality of his films but also reinforced his belief in the communal nature of storytelling.

Redford's work behind the camera also tied closely to his efforts in founding and nurturing the Sundance Institute and Film Festival. While the festival is often discussed separately from his directing career, the two are deeply intertwined. His experience as a director reinforced his understanding of how vital it was to support emerging voices in filmmaking, particularly those outside the Hollywood mainstream. By creating Sundance, he gave independent filmmakers a platform to showcase their work, experiment with form and content, and reach audiences who craved stories that were fresh, daring, and diverse. Sundance became not only a launchpad for new talent but also a cultural touchstone that reshaped the American film landscape, proving that there was room for films made with passion and authenticity, even if they lacked big studio backing.

As the years passed, Redford's directorial projects continued to reflect his evolving interests and his steadfast belief in meaningful storytelling. In *The Horse Whisperer* (1998), which he both directed and starred in, he explored themes of healing, connection, and the bond between humans and animals. The film combined his love for rural landscapes with his skill in crafting emotionally resonant narratives. While critics offered mixed reviews, audiences embraced the film, and it further cemented Redford's reputation as a filmmaker unafraid to merge personal passion with cinematic storytelling.

In many ways, Redford's directing career has been as defining as his acting, if not more so in certain respects. While his iconic performances made him a household name, his work behind the camera revealed the depth of his artistry and his commitment to using film as a tool for reflection and change. He avoided the trap of vanity projects, never relying on his own fame to justify a film's existence. Instead, he consistently pursued stories that mattered to him, stories that engaged with the human condition, with history, with morality, and with the natural world.

His directing success also speaks to a larger truth about Robert Redford: he has always been an artist unwilling to be boxed in by expectations. Hollywood might have preferred him to remain the golden leading man, but he refused to stay still, instead pushing into new territories and proving that his talents were multifaceted. This restless creativity has allowed him to leave a mark not just as an actor but as one of the most thoughtful and enduring filmmakers of his generation.

The Birth of Sundance Film Festival

The birth of the Sundance Film Festival is a story that intertwines Robert Redford's personal vision, his deep commitment to independent voices in cinema, and his enduring belief that film has the power to shift perspectives and create dialogue. To understand how Sundance came into being, one must first appreciate the backdrop of Redford's career during the 1970s and 1980s. By that time, he had already established himself as one of Hollywood's most bankable stars and was experimenting with directing, but he had also grown increasingly dissatisfied with the dominance of big studios and the way they often restricted creativity in favor of commercial safety. Redford was a star, but he was never fully comfortable with the machinery of Hollywood, where financial gain frequently outweighed risk-taking artistry. He had seen firsthand how many daring voices and fresh perspectives were being ignored or shut out because they didn't fit the mold of what executives thought audiences wanted. This discontent simmered in him for years until it began to manifest into something larger—an effort to create a space where independent filmmakers could not only survive but thrive.

The seeds of Sundance were planted in the late 1960s when Redford purchased land in the mountains of Utah. He built a home and established the Sundance Institute, naming it after his famous character, the Sundance Kid. For him, Sundance wasn't merely a retreat from Hollywood but a sanctuary for ideas and creativity. The wilderness and solitude of Utah offered the perfect environment for reflection, experimentation, and growth. Redford's belief was that by nurturing new talent away from the pressures of Hollywood, filmmakers could find their authentic voices. This philosophy was deeply rooted in his own life, shaped by his early struggles, his love for art, and his rebellion against the conformity he often faced in the studio system.

By the early 1980s, Redford realized that while the Sundance Institute was providing workshops and labs to support young filmmakers, there was still a crucial gap. Independent films had limited opportunities to be seen, let alone distributed. Without an audience, the work remained invisible. Redford understood that independent cinema needed not only incubation but also exposure. This realization led to the founding of what would become the Sundance Film Festival. Initially, the festival began in 1978 under a different name, the Utah/US Film Festival, with the purpose of drawing attention to American films and encouraging filmmakers to shoot in Utah. Its early years were modest, and despite some interesting entries, the festival lacked identity and failed to gain traction. But Redford, recognizing its potential, stepped in and took control. He envisioned it not just as a local showcase but as a national and eventually global platform for independent cinema.
In 1984, the Utah/US Film Festival was rebranded under the Sundance name, giving it a new identity and linking it to Redford's vision and reputation. The rebranding was more than cosmetic; it marked a shift in focus, positioning the festival as a place for independent voices, unconventional stories, and daring new filmmakers. Redford emphasized that Sundance would be a festival that valued authenticity over formula, creativity over predictability, and truth over spectacle. By attaching his own credibility to the festival, Redford gave it legitimacy, attracting both filmmakers eager for a chance to be seen and audiences curious about fresh cinematic perspectives.
The birth of the Sundance Film Festival marked a turning point in American cinema. Through Sundance, filmmakers who might have been ignored by mainstream studios suddenly had a stage. The festival quickly became a launchpad for emerging talent, catapulting the careers of directors such as Steven Soderbergh, Quentin Tarantino, Robert Rodriguez, and the Coen brothers. Films like sex, lies, and videotape and Reservoir Dogs found their first audiences at Sundance, proving that independent cinema could not only succeed but also challenge the mainstream. What began as a modest effort to provide a home for indie films became a cultural phenomenon, reshaping the industry and expanding the possibilities of what films could be.
Redford's role in all of this was not merely symbolic. He was deeply involved, advocating for the festival's independence and resisting the pressure to let it become another glamorous Hollywood showcase. He insisted that Sundance maintain its integrity, a place

where films were judged by their originality and impact rather than by star power or budgets. His insistence on this principle kept Sundance distinct from other festivals like Cannes or Venice. While those festivals carried prestige, Sundance carried a sense of rebellion and discovery. It became synonymous with authenticity and risk-taking, echoing Redford's own values.

What made Sundance unique was its environment as much as its programming. The snow-covered mountains of Park City, Utah, created a stark contrast to the glitz of Los Angeles or New York. This setting stripped away some of the pretension associated with film festivals, fostering an atmosphere of intimacy where filmmakers and audiences could interact directly. Redford understood the symbolic power of the place, isolated, quiet, yet invigorating. It reflected his belief that creativity flourished best when freed from distractions and pressures. The physical environment of Sundance became as integral to the festival's identity as the films themselves. As the years went by, Sundance continued to grow in influence. By the 1990s, it had become the premiere venue for independent films, shaping the trajectory of cinema in profound ways. Studios began paying attention, buying up distribution rights to Sundance hits, and adapting their strategies to accommodate the growing popularity of independent films. This evolution was not without challenges. With increasing attention came the danger of commercialization, and critics often pointed out that Sundance risked becoming the very thing it sought to challenge. Redford remained vigilant, pushing back against these tendencies and reminding everyone of the festival's founding principles. Though it could not entirely escape commercialization, Sundance managed to retain its identity as a champion of independent voices, in large part because of Redford's guiding hand.

The birth of Sundance was not just about film; it was about creating a cultural movement. Redford understood that cinema had the potential to inspire empathy, ignite social change, and connect people across divides. Many of the films showcased at Sundance tackled themes and perspectives often absent from mainstream movies—stories about marginalized communities, controversial issues, and daring artistic experiments. In this way, the festival helped broaden the scope of what audiences considered cinema and legitimized voices that otherwise might have been silenced. Redford's commitment to this vision made Sundance more than an event; it became a platform for dialogue, diversity, and artistic courage.

What started as an effort to support struggling filmmakers has grown into a global phenomenon, influencing not just American cinema but also international filmmaking. Filmmakers from around the world now flock to Park City, eager to showcase their work, while audiences see Sundance as a place where innovation thrives. Its success also inspired the growth of independent film festivals worldwide, proving that Redford's model could resonate across cultures.

Reflecting on the birth of Sundance is to reflect on Robert Redford himself. His vision, shaped by his own experiences in Hollywood, his love of art, and his appreciation for authenticity, gave rise to a festival that transformed cinema. Sundance embodies his belief in the power of storytelling, his dedication to nurturing new talent, and his resistance to conformity. It is both a reflection of his personal values and a gift to the filmmaking community at large. Without his leadership, it is unlikely that independent cinema would hold the place it does today in cultural and industry conversations.

Awards and Recognitions

One of Redford's earliest brushes with major recognition came with his role in "Butch Cassidy and the Sundance Kid" in 1969, a film that not only catapulted him to stardom but also drew the attention of critics and award organizations. While the film itself garnered multiple Academy Award nominations, Redford's name became linked to quality, charisma, and a fresh kind of screen presence. Just a few years later, his performance in "The Sting" (1973) earned him an Academy Award nomination for Best Actor, solidifying his status as one of Hollywood's most bankable and respected stars. That nomination was particularly significant because it came during a time when he was at the height of his fame, sharing the screen with Paul Newman again and helping to create one of the most beloved films of its era.

Though he never won a competitive Oscar for acting, Redford's journey with the Academy would continue in even more meaningful ways. His transition into directing proved to be a turning point, as his debut feature film behind the camera, "Ordinary People" (1980), stunned audiences and critics alike with its depth, subtlety, and emotional power. The film won four Academy Awards, including Best Picture, and Redford himself was honored with the Oscar for Best Director. This moment cemented his reputation not just as a talented actor but as a filmmaker of extraordinary skill and vision. The award was particularly symbolic because it represented his ability to step beyond the screen persona that had defined his earlier career and to establish himself as a multifaceted artist. Over the years, Redford would continue to garner recognition from the Academy. In 2002, he received an Honorary Academy Award for his "inspiration to independent and innovative filmmakers everywhere." This award was a nod not only to his contributions as a performer and director but also to his creation of the Sundance Institute and Film Festival, which had by then become one of the most important platforms for independent cinema worldwide. It was an acknowledgment that his influence extended far beyond his own career and touched the broader landscape of filmmaking itself.

The Golden Globe Awards have also played a notable role in honoring Redford's work. Early in his career, he won a Golden Globe for New Star of the Year in 1966 for his performance in "Inside Daisy Clover." This recognition marked him as a rising star in Hollywood, a prediction that would soon come to fruition. Later, his directing work on "Ordinary People" earned him a Golden Globe for Best Director, further aligning his reputation as a serious filmmaker. Over time, he received several nominations from the Hollywood Foreign Press Association, which underscored his long-standing presence in the industry.

In addition to the Oscars and Golden Globes, Redford has been recognized by the British Academy of Film and Television Arts (BAFTA), the Directors Guild of America (DGA), and other prestigious institutions. His honors from these organizations not only celebrate individual performances or films but also reinforce the consistency and longevity of his contributions. Awards from the DGA, in particular, highlight the respect he earned among fellow filmmakers, who admired his ability to craft emotionally resonant and technically proficient stories.

Beyond film industry awards, Robert Redford has also received recognition of a broader cultural nature. In 1996, he was awarded the National Medal of Arts by President Bill Clinton, the highest award given to artists and arts patrons by the United States government. This distinction acknowledged not only his artistic accomplishments but also his work as a champion of independent filmmaking and environmental causes. His influence was seen as stretching into the cultural fabric of America itself. Later, in 2005, Redford was honored with the Kennedy Center Honors, which are awarded annually to individuals who have made significant contributions to American culture through the performing arts. This recognition placed him alongside the most revered cultural icons in the nation, acknowledging both his artistic brilliance and his enduring impact.

Internationally, Redford has also been celebrated. In 2010, French President Nicolas Sarkozy presented him with the Legion of Honor, France's highest distinction. The award symbolized how his influence and contributions resonated beyond American borders, reaching a global audience and affirming the universal appeal of his work both in front of and behind the camera. This recognition was not only a personal accolade but also a reflection of the cross-cultural power of cinema and the way Redford's films spoke to people around the world.

Another notable recognition came when Time magazine named him one of the "100 Most Influential People in the World," a title that reflected not just his cinematic contributions but also his work in environmental activism and his role in shaping independent film. Such acknowledgments illustrate that Redford's legacy is far larger than awards on a shelf; his life's work has rippled outward, influencing culture, politics, art, and global awareness.

Over the decades, Redford has also been the recipient of numerous lifetime achievement awards, which often serve as capstones for remarkable careers. These honors, given by film festivals, guilds, and cultural organizations, emphasize the way he has inspired generations of filmmakers, actors, and audiences. They also serve to remind the public that his achievements cannot be summed up by a single role or film but rather must be viewed as part of a tapestry of contributions across multiple fields.

While many actors and directors achieve recognition in bursts, peaks of fame tied to particular projects Redford's awards and honors illustrate something different: a sustained presence at the highest levels of artistic and cultural contribution. From the fresh-faced actor who first won over critics in the 1960s, to the commanding director of the 1980s, to the elder statesman of cinema and champion of independent voices in the decades since, his accolades track a career that has constantly evolved without ever losing its significance.

Chapter 4

Personal Life and Interests

At the heart of Redford's personal life is his dedication to family. He married Lola Van Wagenen in 1958, long before he achieved fame. Their relationship was rooted in youthful love and shared ideals, and together they raised four children: Scott, Shauna, David James, and Amy. Their marriage lasted nearly three decades, and though it eventually ended in divorce in 1985, the bond they created in building a family remained significant in Redford's life. His experiences as a husband and father grounded him in ways that Hollywood could not. Yet family life was not without its share of heartbreak. The couple's first child, Scott, died tragically as an infant from sudden infant death syndrome, a loss that left a permanent scar on Redford. He rarely spoke publicly about it, but those close to him knew it was an event that shaped his perspective on life and deepened his empathy for the human condition. Redford's other children went on to pursue their own paths, some connected to the arts and others more private, and through them, he found both pride and challenges. Later in life, he married Sibylle Szaggars, a German-born artist, in 2009 after more than a decade of partnership. With Sibylle, Redford seemed to find a companion who shared not only his personal values but also his love for art and the natural world.

Beyond family, Redford's interests have been incredibly wide-ranging, reflecting his restless curiosity and passion for creativity. A lover of painting and drawing since childhood, he often spoke about how art gave him a sense of identity when he was young. Even as acting became his career, painting and visual art never lost their place in his heart. He continued to draw and paint privately, finding in it a meditative escape from the pressures of filmmaking. This affinity for art extended beyond his own creations to his appreciation for others' work. His later relationship with Sibylle, who is herself an accomplished artist, further deepened his immersion in the artistic world, as the two often collaborated on projects blending environmental themes with creative expression.

Nature has always been a central element in Redford's personal life. Raised in Southern California but drawn to open spaces, he sought places of solitude far removed from the frenzy of Hollywood. His purchase of land in Utah during the 1960s was not just a real estate decision but a personal retreat where he could find peace and connection with the wilderness. That land later became the foundation for Sundance, but initially, it was simply his sanctuary. Redford often described nature as restorative, a place where he could think clearly and recharge. Hiking, skiing, and exploring the outdoors became part of his regular routine, not merely hobbies but essential practices for maintaining balance. His advocacy for environmental causes was rooted in this personal bond with the land. Protecting the environment was not just a political stance but an extension of his lifestyle and values.

Another defining aspect of Redford's interests is his commitment to social and political issues. While he never styled himself as a conventional activist, he consistently used his platform to raise awareness about topics close to his heart. From early in his career, he was outspoken about conservation, Native American rights, government transparency, and the need for independent voices in media and film. His political views leaned progressive, but he preferred action over rhetoric. This is perhaps why he invested so heavily in building institutions like the Sundance Institute, which gave filmmakers tools rather than simply words of encouragement. Redford's engagement with politics also showed in his film choices, as he gravitated toward projects that dealt with issues like Watergate, corruption, environmental destruction, and the complexities of American society.

Though his interests in art, politics, and the environment were serious, Redford was never without a sense of adventure and appreciation for leisure. He loved sports, particularly baseball, which he played in his youth. In fact, his passion for the game was evident in his performance in The Natural, where his ease on the field reflected a lifetime of affection for the sport. He also enjoyed skiing, a pastime perfectly aligned with his love for Utah's mountains. Redford was known to retreat to the slopes not only for recreation but also as a way to stay active and connected with the outdoors.

In his personal relationships, Redford has often been described as private, sometimes even reserved, but those who knew him well paint a portrait of a man deeply loyal to his friends and collaborators. He valued meaningful connections over superficial ones and built lifelong bonds with many people in the film industry. Despite his fame, he disliked the trappings of celebrity culture and resisted being labeled as just another Hollywood star. This aversion to celebrity was perhaps why he lived much of his life outside of Los Angeles, preferring Utah or other quieter places where he could feel more human and less defined by the industry.

Redford's later years have shown a man who, while slowing down from the pace of his acting and directing, never stopped engaging with the world. He continued to support Sundance and environmental initiatives, to spend time with family, and to immerse himself in creative projects, whether through film, art, or writing. He cultivated a personal philosophy rooted in independence, creativity, and a responsibility to give back, both to his community and to the larger world. His life outside the screen has been marked not by scandal or spectacle, but by a quiet resilience and a dedication to living authentically.

Activism and Environmental Work

Redford's earliest activism can be traced back to the late 1960s and 1970s, a time when the environmental movement was only beginning to gain momentum. At a time when most Hollywood stars were primarily concerned with their next role, Redford was speaking out against unchecked development and environmental destruction. He lent his growing fame and credibility to causes that many in the entertainment world ignored. He recognized the power of celebrity to shine a light on issues that might otherwise remain in the shadows, but he approached this responsibility with sincerity rather than self-promotion. Redford often said that his connection to the environment was personal before it became political; he wasn't just supporting abstract ideals but fighting to preserve the landscapes that inspired his creativity and nourished his sense of self.

One of his most significant contributions has been his long-standing partnership with the Natural Resources Defense Council (NRDC), an organization dedicated to protecting the Earth's environment through science, law, and advocacy. Redford became one of the most visible advocates for the NRDC, using his platform to highlight issues ranging from clean air and water to wildlife conservation and climate change. For decades, he appeared in campaigns, wrote articles, narrated documentaries, and even participated in lobbying efforts to influence policy. Unlike many celebrities who attach their names to causes for brief publicity, Redford's involvement has been sustained, deep, and impactful, reflecting his genuine dedication to environmental protection.

The creation of the Sundance Institute and later the Sundance Film Festival also tie into Redford's broader vision of activism. While these endeavors are primarily associated with independent filmmaking, they also represent his belief in nurturing voices that could tell stories often ignored by mainstream culture. Many of these stories, especially over the years, have tackled themes of environmental justice, climate change, and humanity's relationship with nature. Through Sundance, Redford provided a platform not only for artists but also for activists who use film as a tool for awareness and change. In this sense, his activism and artistic legacy are intertwined, each reinforcing the other.

Redford has also been vocal about political issues, particularly when they intersect with environmental concerns. He was an early critic of fossil fuel dependency and one of the prominent voices warning against the dangers of climate change long before it became a global emergency. He repeatedly criticized governmental inaction, urging leaders to take bold steps in the fight against environmental degradation. Whether it was testifying before Congress, writing op-eds in major newspapers, or speaking at international forums, Redford did not shy away from the political dimensions of environmentalism. His words carried weight not just because of his fame, but because of the consistency and depth of his commitment.

One of the areas closest to his heart has been the American West, particularly Utah, where he has lived for much of his life. He fought tirelessly to protect its natural beauty from overdevelopment, mining, and exploitation. Redford was particularly concerned with the preservation of public lands and national parks, which he viewed as treasures belonging to all people and future generations. He supported campaigns to expand protections for these areas and opposed legislation that threatened them. For him, this was not only an ecological battle but also a cultural one: preserving the landscapes of the West was about maintaining the soul of America, a place where wilderness could inspire imagination, resilience, and a sense of connection to the planet.

Redford's activism was not without risk. Speaking out on controversial issues, particularly environmental regulation and energy policy, often put him at odds with powerful industries and political figures. Yet he remained steadfast, unwilling to compromise his principles for the sake of popularity or convenience. In doing so, he helped pave the way for other artists and celebrities to use their platforms for advocacy, setting an example that fame can be a tool for meaningful change.

Beyond policy and advocacy, Redford also emphasized the importance of education in environmental work. He believed that true change required not just laws and regulations but also a shift in public consciousness. To this end, he supported educational programs, funded initiatives aimed at raising awareness among young people, and consistently spoke about the need for cultural transformation in how society views the natural world. He often stressed that the environment was not a distant concern but something that affected everyday life, health, and community well-being.

As technology advanced and new environmental challenges emerged, Redford adapted his activism to address them. He spoke out about global warming, renewable energy, and sustainable living, always highlighting the interconnectedness of environmental health and human prosperity. He warned that the costs of ignoring environmental degradation would be severe, not just for nature but for economies, societies, and future generations. His words resonated because they were rooted not in abstract ideology but in lived experience and heartfelt conviction.

Redford's environmental work also extended internationally. He participated in global conversations on climate change, lending his voice to campaigns that reached audiences far beyond the United States. He used his influence to draw attention to the urgency of international cooperation, emphasizing that environmental problems know no borders. His advocacy helped bridge the gap between scientific research and public awareness, translating complex issues into compelling narratives that could inspire action.

Perhaps one of the most remarkable aspects of Redford's activism is how seamlessly it coexists with his identity as an artist. Unlike those who treat activism as separate from their professional lives, Redford integrated his values into his art. His films often carried subtle but powerful messages about humanity's relationship with nature, the consequences of greed and exploitation, and the importance of integrity and courage. In this way, he demonstrated that storytelling could be a form of activism, shaping public consciousness and inspiring reflection.

Even as he aged and stepped back from the spotlight of acting, Redford continued to speak out on environmental issues. His voice, steady and passionate, remained a guiding force for activists and ordinary citizens alike. For many, his advocacy became as iconic as his film roles, solidifying his reputation not just as a Hollywood legend but as a moral leader. His work reminds us that celebrity is fleeting, but the impact of using one's influence for good can be lasting.

Robert Redford's Impact on Hollywood and the World

When Redford first began his career in the 1960s, Hollywood was in the midst of change. The studio system that had defined the Golden Age of cinema was crumbling, and audiences were demanding films that felt more authentic, grounded, and relevant to their lives. Redford entered this landscape with a unique blend of all-American charm and a natural, understated talent. His early work in films such as "Barefoot in the Park" and "Butch Cassidy and the Sundance Kid" established him not only as a bankable star but as a new kind of leading man one who embodied both rugged masculinity and a quiet, introspective sensitivity. His ability to bring depth to his roles helped redefine what it meant to be a Hollywood star in an era when audiences were craving authenticity.

As his career grew, Redford became part of a new wave of actors who elevated storytelling in film, choosing projects that challenged audiences rather than simply entertaining them. In "The Candidate," for instance, he explored the corrupting influence of politics, while in "All the President's Men," he embodied investigative journalist Bob Woodward, capturing the dogged persistence that helped uncover the Watergate scandal. These roles were more than just performances; they mirrored the anxieties and aspirations of a society grappling with distrust in government and a hunger for truth. In playing such roles, Redford helped usher in an era where movies could be both commercially successful and politically relevant.

Redford's influence, however, was not limited to his acting. His transition into directing marked another chapter in his impact on Hollywood. His debut as a director with "Ordinary People" in 1980 stunned critics and audiences alike, not only because the film was so emotionally powerful but because it revealed a new side of Redford. He demonstrated that his talents extended well beyond the camera's lens and into the realm of storytelling from the director's chair. "Ordinary People" won four Academy Awards, including Best Picture and Best Director for Redford, establishing him as a filmmaker with a gift for exploring the complexity of human relationships. Through his directing, Redford became known for prioritizing character-driven narratives, creating films that emphasized subtle emotional truths over spectacle. This focus would influence generations of filmmakers who followed.

Yet perhaps Redford's most enduring contribution to Hollywood is the creation of the Sundance Film Festival. What began as a small event in Utah in the late 1970s evolved into the world's premier showcase for independent cinema. At a time when major studios dominated the industry and smaller voices struggled to be heard, Redford recognized the need for a platform where innovative, risk-taking films could find an audience. Sundance became that space, giving rise to filmmakers such as Quentin Tarantino, Steven Soderbergh, and the Coen brothers, all of whom got their start at the festival. By championing independent film, Redford helped diversify the cinematic landscape, ensuring that Hollywood was not the sole arbiter of what stories could be told. His work with Sundance has given countless filmmakers the opportunity to share their unique visions, reshaping not only American cinema but global storytelling. Beyond the screen, Redford's activism further solidified his influence on the world. Long before environmentalism became mainstream, Redford was advocating for conservation and raising awareness about climate change, renewable energy, and the preservation of natural landscapes. He used his celebrity status to amplify these causes, writing, speaking, and producing films and documentaries that brought pressing environmental issues into public discourse. His work with organizations like the Natural Resources Defense Council and his dedication to protecting wilderness areas cemented his reputation as an activist who did not simply lend his name to causes but worked tirelessly to effect real change. His ability to bridge art and activism showed that cultural figures could wield their influence responsibly, making a tangible difference in society.

On the international stage, Redford became a symbol of the socially conscious artist. His films, his festival, and his advocacy inspired not only Americans but people worldwide to reconsider the role of art in addressing pressing societal issues. He demonstrated that cinema could function as both entertainment and activism, capable of sparking conversations and influencing public opinion. The global reach of the Sundance Film Festival ensured that independent voices from across the world could share their stories, fostering cultural exchange and broadening perspectives. In this sense, Redford's influence transcended Hollywood and became part of a larger movement toward using storytelling as a tool for global understanding and empathy.

Redford's impact is also deeply personal for those who grew up watching his films or discovered their love of cinema through Sundance. He redefined the possibilities of what film could accomplish, showing that actors could be more than celebrities, that directors could be truth-tellers, and that festivals could be platforms for social and artistic revolutions. By living a life that consistently merged creativity with conscience, he set a standard for artists who aspire to make a difference both in their field and in the world.

It is also worth noting that Redford's impact was achieved without the trappings of loud self-promotion or relentless pursuit of fame. He carried himself with quiet dignity, often retreating to his ranch in Utah to focus on his art and his activism rather than seeking constant media attention. This authenticity resonated with audiences and gave him a credibility that few in Hollywood could match. His career stands as proof that one can achieve lasting success without compromising integrity or vision.

Printed in Dunstable, United Kingdom